TABLE OF CONTENTS

Introduction v

LETTER 1: Save America 1

LETTER 2: Abandoned Mother 3

LETTER 3: Tired 5

LETTER 4: I Miss My Mom 7

LETTER 5: Troubled Mind 9

LETTER 6: So, About this Fathering Issue 13

LETTER 7: I Can Still Feel Their Hands on Me 17

LETTER 8: You Are Prized by Majesty 19

LETTER 9: I'm Scared! 21

LETTER 10: He Stole My Innocence 23

LETTER 11: You Didn't Let Me See This One 25

LETTER 12: The Purpose of Pain 29

LETTER 13: Relentless Love 31

LETTER 14: Forgiveness is Overrated 35

LETTER 15: Unwanted Anger 37

LETTER 16: Abandonment Issues 39

LETTER 17: Come Back Home 41

LETTER 18: Sometimes "In" is the "Out" 43

LETTER 19: Trust Me...47

LETTER 20: I Belong to You...51

LETTER 21: I'm Grateful...55

LETTER 22: Daddy Dearest..57

LETTER 23: I'm Holding on to You..59

LETTER 24: No Longer Slaves..61

LETTER 25: I Am Your Sanctuary...63

LETTER 26: Your Coronation..65

LETTER 27: Enter In..67

LETTER 28: Forever to Love You..69

LETTER 29: Affirmed by ABBA...71

PROPHETIC LETTERS

RELEASING THE FATHER'S VOICE
TO AN ORPHANED GENERATION

A COMPILATION BY
LATRICE LEAKE
AND PROPHETIC SCRIBES

Prophetic Letters: Releasing the Father's Voice to an Orphaned Generation Copyright © 2020

A Compilation by Latrice Leake

Published in the United States of America by

ChosenButterflyPublishing LLC

www.cb-publishing.com

All Scripture quotations, unless otherwise indicated, are taken from the Holy Bible, KING JAMES VERSION (KJV): KING JAMES VERSION, public domain.

Scripture quotations marked (NLT) are taken from the Holy Bible, New Living Translation, copyright © 1996, 2004, 2007, 2013, 2015 by Tyndale House Foundation. Used by permission of Tyndale House Publishers, Inc., Carol Stream, Illinois 60188. All rights reserved.

All rights reserved under International Copyright Law. Contents and/or cover may not be reproduced, distributed, or transmitted in any form or by any means or stored in a database or retrieval system without the prior written consent of the publisher and/or authors.

ISBN: 978-1-945377-12-9

First Edition Printing

Printed in the United States of America

2020

INTRODUCTION

The Father speaks and we, the Children of the Lord, hear His voice. Our faintest hearts cries are clearly and loudly heard down the courts and even in the Throne Room of God. Our Father is intent about communicating with us. This book was inspired by the Spirit of the Lord and His intense desire to speak to us amid pain, the busyness of life, and every sound that is contending for our attention. The glaring noise that social media, our bills, education, children, marriage, grief, the past, our careers, and even our future makes; it all tries to drown out the peace that can only be found in the Father's voice, in His love, and in His presence. It is my prayer that you will take a moment to be still long enough to hear the message penned by myself and the co-authors of this prophetic compilation. Each one has sought the Lord, spent time in prayer and fasting, and has also encountered much warfare in order to deliver this message of truth to your hands.

I remember being a little girl and making my friends play church. We would purchase a bag of Bar B Que chips from the corner store, and I would preach to them. It is no surprise that my messages would closely emulate the teachings of my youth pastor. I would pick short, easy-to-remember scriptures of the Lord's unfailing love. The same scripture would always show up in my messages... John 3:16, "For God so loved the world, that he gave his only begotten Son, that whosoever believeth in him should not perish, but have everlasting life." That was always how I ended my messages. The kids would clap, and church would end with a piece of my one slice of pie purchased after my real church service. The church dining hall after church always smelled of delicious hot fried chicken, potato salad, and the best string beans next to your grandmother's. We'd stand in the slowly moving line to get that slice, and I'd carry it home with great care for my after-church service.

It's amazing what the Lord can put in the hearts of children sometimes. My sweet offering was broken and put onto about four or five plastic forks for all of my friends; the same as the body of Christ, broken for us so that we can partake in His body and be saved. Father is still speaking the wonderful story of salvation to us, but beyond even salvation there is more. It's called relationship encounters. He desires to go deeper in relationship with us. He wants to speak the Whys of life to us. He wants to speak His tender heart toward humanity. He doesn't call us orphans, but many have missed the message that we have been adopted and are now the sons of God.

So grab your pen, put on some soaking worship, your prayer journal, and a plastic fork so that you can dig into this offering broken before you. Allow the words to gently rest upon your heart; may they come to you gently like the morning dew, sweetly falling to the earth. This book comes to quench the soul's desire to be heard and to receive from eternity. The crown jewel of Heaven has heard and honored even your unspoken request.

Love,

Prophet Latrice

LATRICE'S ACKNOWLEDGEMENTS

I would like to acknowledge my mother, Ardeen Leake; thank you for every sacrifice and intangible character quality that God used you to cultivate in me since birth. I love you!

To my son, Isaiah Hunter Leake, you have made my life so colorful and full of adventure. I thank God for the incredible prophet, priest, and father that you will be to my grandchildren one day very far in the future. Mommy loves you, my precious son!

To my dad, Apostle Johnny Leake, thank you for loving me. Though the enemy has a way of trying to separate children from the voice of their natural fathers, I'm grateful that you are still here with me to celebrate this victory that God has given us in restoration.

Big Sis, Lachae Leake. I don't know if I know anyone with a heart bigger than yours! You serve everyone. Much love to you, Abraham and the kids!

To my beautiful leaders Pastor Raequael Patterson & Jonathan Patterson thank God for you both!

#LCHSTRONG

To my best friend, Prophet Yolanda Lowery-Cole ... sissssssssyyyyy thank you for sharing this journey with me and for being the person I can share my heart with always. I'm so grateful for you and Pastor Jabari Cole, your beautiful family, and my nephew Nova.

Lakeyla, Bianca, Shalonda, Shetia ... whewww! Thank you, ladies. Lakeyla, you are one of my greatest supporters. You've always cheered my name, pushed and prayed, and I pray that God gives you every desire for your heart.

Apostle Marlon D. Hester, Apostle Michele Pererra, and Sapphire family church. You all have been strategic in my growth as a prophet and in the prophetic. Thank you!

Pastors Jermaine and Talita thank you for being you; authentic, genuine, and displaying the heart of Christ always.

Chanel and Tony Clark ... ya'll! Listen, you guys have ridden so hard for Isaiah and me always. I love you guys!

Thank you to my co-authors, you guys are absolutely a stunning accent to my life. Your light, laughter, humility and gifting are such blessings!

I'm grateful to my Mission Rock family; you guys are rocking and amazing!

Prophet Ayanna and ChosenButterfly Publishing. Thank you for your hard work, your professionalism, and Kingdom excellence. The manner in which you published this work was absolutely refreshing.

Thank you to Dustin Clarity for our beautiful graphics. You are an incredible designer.

Finally, to those who feel abandoned, you are the beloved of our Heavenly Father. He hasn't forgotten you and you've been adopted into the household of faith.

~ Latrice

SAVE AMERICA

Dear God,

It feels like you can't hear me. My cries have gone up before you and have gone unheard, like calls of distress echoing over a desolate city in ruin. No life is where my cries go forth. It feels like we're screaming into the darkness, like the wickedness is towering over our naked bodies bleeding in our streets. The blood of millions of innocents runs down the mountains of the world that you created. The waters have overcome the earth.

We are drowning in despair; our hope has withered to naught. The flag of surrender has been waved, but our enemy has still sought to consume us. Where is rest for the weary soul? Who will save us from the snare of an enemy who hides in the shadows while mothers and fathers die in hospital rooms alone? People gasping for air, crying for a cure, and none is in sight.

They say this country is built on Christian principles, but I have looked for you everywhere and can't seem to find you. Your prayers taken out of schools; lawless and perverse men and women are creating laws and governing our territories. We need an answer! We need you to answer! Give us hope as the days get darker and darker. Give us the ability to see in the dark, to peer through the clouds of despair and wickedness.

The wicked have covered our nation with a cloak of deceit. Will you rescue us? You've paid our ransoms and we have gone back and cut covenant with those you delivered us from. Our addiction to Babylon and Egypt has been our downfall. Save us again, Father!

You're our only hope.

Signed,

~ The United States of America

ABANDONED MOTHER

My first Mother's Day, my son had been in the NICU for almost three weeks. I prayed day and night for him to get better, pumped breast milk, and visited him every day several times a day. It was exhausting, not to mention due to the lack of rest I had pneumonia and my heart was leaking fluid from my valve at the rate of a 70-year-old woman. I hated my baby being in the NICU. Nurses critiquing every move I made, listening to every word I said to my baby, and telling me to put gloves on to touch him. It was a lot. I had to wear a mask because I was on antibiotics. As I was leaving the hospital last MOTHER'S DAY, I saw a family happily taking their baby home. The mother was being carefully pushed in a wheelchair by the baby's father, and I was walking out alone without my baby. I blinked away my hot tears that filled my eyes... It was hard, but God is faithful!

Signed,

~ I Don't Understand

TIRED

Dear God,

As I listen to the sound of the small plastic wheels of my son's toy train rubbing up and down the receptionists' desk at the DNA lab I stand in awe that I'm actually here. After years of trying to dodge a dead-end relationship, traps, and men problems, I'm single with a toddler trying to prove to his father that he is his son and that I deserve help with raising him even if it's just the $150 a month that he used to send me. And while I wear an invincible smile the pain goes deep. Not because I want him but because I did everything that I could to avoid this. I wanted to avoid my son running up to strange men in public, reaching up and calling them Daddy. I tried to keep him from crying when the other kids' dads picked them up from daycare and he would cry to leave with male strangers. I tried to avoid this ugly thief that has robbed us; this ugly generational curse that hit my grandmother, my mom, and now me.

I remember sitting in my room and crying while asking you, "Am I cursed?" The question was as real as I know you are. I asked because my dad never wanted me, and the only memory that I ever had of him was at three when he promised me the red bike with silver pom poms on it. That bike never came, and neither did the love of any man. My biological father married my mother while he was still married, my grandmother found out through her friend of many years, and the only man that I knew as a grandfather we found out at his funeral that he was already married. My grandmother was devastated! I remember as a young girl the look in her eyes when we walked into the funeral and she was escorted to the back with a small mention of her name in the funeral program. This curse followed me as I stand in line with the baby of someone's husband who deceived me, and I took the bait and had a child with him. Wheels creaking in this quiet shameful room, checking in to prove what all parties know is the truth.

I never thought I'd end up here. Never thought I'd be fighting to clear my name. To tell my side of the story, to explain that I tried to reach out to his wife to verify the truth after he told me they were divorced for two years. Those little plastic wheels rolling back and forth on that old wooden desk while my little boy gives me the most beautiful grin. His face is like anesthesia to the pain of this moment.

During the DNA collection we fake like swabbing our jaws is a game and because my son does fun better than anyone, he playfully agrees to this game. He makes eye contact with me and we giggle in between the woman collecting our DNA to submit to the state, almost as if we are invisible and the only ones here. The woman takes our picture and we step back into reality. My son goes to daycare and I go off to work. At the end of the day I'm tired. This event has rocked me, not because I'm weak but because I need help. I'm exhausted down to my soul. I've been crying out for help, but all I keep finding is myself in shameful rooms, trying to prove my innocence. I'm trying to understand why you didn't stop the shame that has happened to the women in my family. We are good women. We didn't deserve this. No one does.

Signed,

~ A Single Mother Who Is Tired

I MISS MY MOM

Orphan—a word I have only thought of on occasion, but not one I would have ever thought that I would have to attribute to myself. It still sounds a bit unnerving when I now must think of myself as an orphan, or should I? When I think of the word orphan, it brings a heaviness to my heart that cannot be explained. I now must consider the word. I must also consider the why. Why do I now after forty-eight years of living find myself without a mother and a father? The loss of my mother I call legitimate. But the loss of my father? Man! I never saw that coming!

I lost my mother to breast cancer after a little over a yearlong fight. Some say she gave up, but I say she retired gracefully. Some may not agree, but that's my opinion. My mother was a woman of great pride in her ability to care for her husband and her home. You would never find her home dirty. Everything was always in its proper place. But after a heart attack and five strokes, her mind and body just couldn't keep up with the daily task of keeping her home in the manner she was accustomed to. After a while, it depressed her and she was just ready to go meet her savior face-to-face. I still remember when the nurse had said she could go at any time. I said, "Mama, the nurse said the Lord will be coming to get you anytime now." At this time, she was no longer speaking, but I saw her blush after having no color for days. I believe that was when she must have seen an angel or the Lord because she was gone after that. My best friend left and didn't take me with her. I was left behind, but I still had my father—or did I? I believe when she died, he died with her.

My dad, who I said died with my mother, is yet still living. But I don't know him. He has become the opposite of everything he and my mother taught us to be. He began doing all the things that we got punished for as young adults. He began doing the things that would have gotten us thrown in the middle of a prayer circle with oil put on us to cleanse us from evil. He was unrecognizable, full of pride, and spoke of all his money and how he did it all. How could he now leave out God? He taught us that everything came from God and that it was God and he alone provides for us. How? How could he now talk and act like King Nebuchadnezzar in the book of Daniel, full of pride? He was now wearing his hair long in a ponytail, which reminded me of when Nebuchadnezzar was turned into a wild person with all that hair. Jesus! Who was this man and where did my father go? What happened to him or was he like this all along hiding under the skirt of my mother? He betrayed us all, my brother and sisters. I cannot speak about it because you know it's those things families just don't talk about.

In the end, he felt I was being negative about his new life and child bride. Did I say child bride? Yes. It is not because I am angry but because she is younger than my eldest son. He told me not to call him and blocked my number. I did manage to tell him I loved him before he hung up. But on that day, I became an orphan. My mother was gone and now my father. The only father I knew was gone.

So yes, I am now that word, orphan. I say it's no big deal but, wow! I am an orphan. A word I never would have thought I would attribute to myself, but I am alright. I tell myself, "I am alright."

Signed,

~ I am alright

TROUBLED MIND

I'm in conflict. I don't like people. I don't trust people. Their words and their actions mean nothing right now. My natural feeling is to avoid people altogether. That has become my way of coping with life. I can't live isolated forever, which is why I'm coming to you.

My heart is hurting. My soul is aching. Father, I still feel the pain of the moment when I was raped. Even years later, it still plagues me in ways unimaginable. I've struggled with forgiveness and trust for years. I can't forgive someone who violated me in the worst way possible. My right to refuse sexual intercourse was taken from me. Someone overpowered me and robbed me of my innocence. Someone I trusted to protect me exerted authority over me and left me powerless. They were supposed to shield me but instead forced me to accept a diet that no child should ever experience.

Help me to undo the power of feeling vulnerable and exposed to the world. Father, help me to break this allegiance with hatred towards my family. They should have known that something was wrong, but instead they did nothing. My family was supposed to defend me. Instead, I was ridiculed when I acted out the effects of actions taken against me.

Lord, how do I learn to forgive? How do I heal? My heart aches for freedom from the demons of days past. I don't want to live my life in constant fear of the unknown. I don't want to live as a victim. That demeanor doesn't fit my future.

This isn't just rehearsing the events but a craving for retaliation. I'm angry and I want them to pay—equally, if not worse. Violence isn't how you suggest that we handle these situations. I don't know any other way to express the content in my heart aside from being angry. Plus, violence wouldn't solve anything. Father, HELP ME! The sight of familiar faces sends me into a rage. I'm not an angry person at my core. Yet the strength to fight that I needed in my adolescence wants to surface in my adulthood.

Your eyes are everywhere. You see all things. Did you not see me in distress? Did you not see me fighting for my life? I'm tired of reimagining the day I was left in a pool of my own blood. If your son' blood redeems me, can you exchange mine for His? Can His blood restore what I lost?

I still struggle to defeat the memories of that day. I was left to make sense of this violence by myself. Will this nightmare end? Will I ever experience what every person dreams of having—true love? I want a love that isn't violent but carries the gentlest and firmest of embraces.

I've tried to love beyond this. Every relationship I've been in has centered on sex. Perhaps it's the broken parts of my life being exploited again. I don't know anything aside from offering my body as an expression of love. Yes, that is skewed, but it's a truth that is present with me. Father, teach me to love myself first before anyone. Teach me the value of love as you've designed it. Thank you.

I have to learn to forgive you most importantly. I can't reconcile how you could let me lie hopeless in despair. I know you as a father, but I struggle with forgiving you. I've never felt so naked, so exposed. Uncovered, even. My natural family didn't believe my truth. Now I tell you the truth and I hope that you will act upon it. I was the innocent party. I didn't bring this on myself. I wish people would understand that.

You see me where I am. You know that my present reality is not what was imagined for me. If you're able, please help.

Signed,

~ Hopeless in a timewarp

SO, ABOUT THIS FATHERING ISSUE

Good morning, Lord.

So many men have made promises to me. None of them have lived up to their word which makes everyone questionable. I've started to live with this suspicion that the next person is the same as the last person, just in a different form.

Men that I connect to often ask questions about my upbringing. I'm not ashamed to tell some of my truth, I feel like that gives context as to the person I am today. I know that somewhere within they can hear the longing for connectivity. I don't try to overemphasize this, it just radiates naturally.

I have yet to encounter anyone who can understand the plight that I face. I feel like an orphan who has been abandoned by all of society. I heard some of the seniors say that it takes a village to raise a child. If this is true, then where is my village? Where are those who will be my barrier and shield me from veering into destructive paths? I don't have anyone, honestly. Yes, I have friends, but even they are only relevant until their next score comes along.

Lord, I don't fit into any one particular circle. You didn't design humans to exist independent of each other. How will I learn to appreciate a community if I don't feel safe with people? I feel like I have only a few moments until I'm dropped again.

It pains me to see others around me mistreat their parents. They have the one thing that I want more than anything: both parents alive. I try not to get angry, but I can't help it.

All I've wanted is to feel like I belong to a family. I want to feel like I matter to people. More specifically, I want to belong to a father. I want someone to claim me as their own. I want to feel protected. I long for those moments when I can call and talk to a father for wisdom and knowledge about life. I long for those moments when I can open my heart to a male senior and not feel forced to be anything except a son in need. I long to create memories with my dad and strengthen the bond between us.

I honestly feel that there's no need to try this narrative again. It ends up being a repeat of the last disaster, except with different faces. My patience is wearing thin, Lord. I'm almost ready to just isolate myself from the world. I don't think my request is that extreme. I really just want to fit in without fear of retaliation or abuse of my time or emotions.

Trying to connect with people is so exhausting. Then, when I do connect, the people around that paternal figure become jealous and extremely cold. You would think that I had slapped them or something. Surely this can't be what you expect from "church people"? They look past me and walk by as if I don't exist. That can't be how we're supposed to treat each other if we're supposed to be Christians.

I have to admit that it isn't just church people either. Humanity has this issue bad. People want me to change myself to fit into a mold that isn't designed for me. It almost feels like I'm forcing myself to make these unnecessary adjustments or trying to justify these actions.

Someone once told me that a true son will always make their father look exemplary. So I tried to alter my speech, my behavior and the way I dress. They said, "Make sure you aren't doing too much or too little." It's so unnatural having to adjust for the sake of people.

Why do I have to 'become' something I'm not? I'm not the perfect person. I have my shortcomings. I still make mistakes. I feel like a real father wouldn't judge me for being flawed. They would accept me as I am without pretense. Have I been lied to or have I adopted these false expectations of myself? Was the role of a father misrepresented to me or am I treating this invisible mentor like a Build-A-Bear?

Signed,

~ I'm tired.

I CAN STILL FEEL THEIR HANDS ON ME

Dear God,

Every time they touched me, I wondered where you were. Prostituted at five years old by my grandmother, molested by my stepfather and other strangers, raped at 14—what kind of life is that to live? For years I heard spiritual leaders tell me that it had to be so, so that you could get the glory out of my life. That never sat well with me. Does that mean you authorized every touch and rape? How does that help anyone see you as good? There has to be more to the story.

Every time it happened I cried out internally for you until it happened so often I just stopped crying at all. A part of me died each time. I resigned myself to the shadows and attached to myself the belief that this was both love and unworthiness. In other words, love will always hurt, and I should accept whatever form it comes in because I am clearly not worthy of protection. So I yielded to whatever abuse was inflicted upon me every single day. I had no voice, and I had no support.

I wish I could say I left that feeling behind in childhood. I wish I could say that by some amazing influence I grew up to become a whole and healthy, well-adjusted individual. I think I have even led myself to believe that there is some truth to that, but the facts are glaring in almost every life choice I have made since those childhood times. The fact that I am still worthless is reflected in every relationship I've had. I have had men and women and still the result is the same. I am not sure what I am looking for, but I have met failure after failure and I am tired.

There's this scripture that talks about every time you want to do right evil is always present (Romans 7:21). Is that the fate I am resigned to? On the outside I excel. I am successful and have made a pretty decent life for myself, but in love and sex I fail every time. What am I looking for? What am I projecting? I feel like I should be stronger. I have this "great call" on my life, but this internal sexual battle at the same time. I can't go forward in this condition. It's the same story, just different characters, and where there are no physical characters there is porn and an addiction to it to boot. I am tired of this struggle, tired of being alone and sexless, and tired of hearing that I should just hold on and trust you. I am humiliated and embarrassed. I don't want to keep pretending I am okay only to have my heart broken again.

Signed,

~ Afraid to trust again

YOU ARE PRIZED BY MAJESTY

Dear Son / Daughter,

I know it's been hard to find me through the craziness of life. I know it's been hard to believe in my promises with all the darkness that you've encountered. In fact, I know that you've even begun to lose faith in me. You feel like I haven't been there ... like I abandoned you. You feel like I disappeared when you needed me most. The people I sent to encourage you didn't really make much of an impact and you feel like you're drowning in the sea of life.

I had to step back to develop you. Why? Let me tell you. There's so much in you that you can't see. There's an untapped strength and resilience in you. There's a greater ability in you and I had to step back to allow you to see that. Reflect on the things that have happened in your life and see that the moments that produced the greatest parts of you are the moments when you felt alone. I chose to do it this way because I wanted to show you that you didn't need anyone, but me, to be strong. You don't have to rely on anyone. When I created you, I created you with everything you need inside of you and I developed those things through tests.

I want you to lift your head. You are not weak! You are not defeated! You are not going to die here. On the contrary, this is the time for you to live. I want you to live boldly and live freely. I see you emerging as a force in the earth. I need you to understand that I DESIRE YOU TO LIVE! As you live, learn. And as you learn, grow! This season has been one of extreme testing, I know that; but I still purposed it. My desire is that you will be able to recognize it and come into the strength of my will.

I never left you and I never will. I need you to know that. I've been here the entire time watching you from the sidelines. Rooting you on. Cheering you on. I was there celebrating every victory and encouraging you through every loss. I'm still here. My son / daughter, you are going to win! You are going to win. Get up, dust yourself off and let's get this victory ... TOGETHER!

~ God

Scriptures:

>Jeremiah 29:11 (NLT) – "'For I know the plans I have for you,' says the Lord. 'They are plans for good and not for disaster, to give you a future and a hope.'"

>Jeremiah 31:3 (NLT) – "Long ago the Lord said to Israel: 'I have loved you, my people, with an everlasting love. With unfailing love, I have drawn you to myself.'"

I'M SCARED!

Dear God,

I just want to feel safe. I thought I was going to feel that today, but there goes that sound again! My mom is screaming because he's beating her. I thought today would be a good day! They were just kissing in the kitchen. Today was supposed to be a good day. I prayed extra hard last night. Did you hear me? To be honest, I get tired of hearing the sound of the doors slamming and things falling. I'm scared that one day he might turn and hit me. Why does she stay? Is she going to die? Will he kill her?

The night I sat in the backseat of the car, next to him, while he ripped the hair from her scalp with his hands, was a lot for me to handle. I still remember the tears falling from her eyes as he did it. I never got over that. It's been etched in my head for over 20 years. I recall how helpless she looked as it happened. I remember the tears that streamed down her face. I wished I could save her. I wanted to help her, but I was too small to do so. Why did that happen? That was the night I stopped feeling safe. Actually, it was the night I stopped being safe. What do you do, as a child, when you no longer feel safe?

The soundtrack of my youth, the time of my innocent, was shattered glass, slammed doors, yelling, punched bodies and screams of pain. While my friends had families that were happy, I was often afraid to go home because I wanted to escape the abuse. Was it my fault that they were fighting? Did I do something? Was it because I wasn't a "straight boy" that she was suffering? What could I do to make it stop? As I sat up in my bed, hearing her say, "Stop. That hurts. Stop!" to no avail I felt helpless. I remember knocking on the door and hearing her struggle through being choked to say, "I'm fine, go back to bed." I tried to believe her and go to bed, but I stayed awake until it was over. I'm unsure of how much time passed before it ended; all I know is that I turned to the wall and played sleep when she came to check on me and my siblings.

Is this the way that love is supposed to be? Can love exist without pain? God, why do people suffer? Will I ever feel safe anywhere?

Signed,

~ Your Child Who Doesn't Know What Safety Is

HE STOLE MY INNOCENCE

Dear God,

Why? Why was this the road that I had to take? Why did I have to deal with this? I heard the preacher say that we all have a "THIS", but why was this my "THIS"? You know what I'm talking about! The thing that my family and the church make me feel embarrassed and ashamed about. The thing that my classmates teased me about and called me before I even knew what - was. Why was this my THIS? You know what it is! I don't even have to say it! The thing that makes me want to kill myself. The thing that was deposited in me by someone who was supposed to love me.

I remember the day THIS thing started. I was home with him, and he touched me. He put THIS here and then left. Then, when others came, they only added to it! Why was this my THIS? I'm angry! I'm confused! Why was this my THIS? Out of all the things I could have struggled with, you gave me THIS! Why THIS? Why ME? It was bad enough that I had to grow up without a father and I was never really able to connect with my male peers; and they labeled me. I was always closer to the girls so that made me one! I was the awkward kid.

I never had anyone to teach me how to play sports. I was always afraid to catch balls. I was frail and wanted to play with dolls. Why was this my THIS? Did you know I would be teased? Did you know I would be ostracized? Did you know? If you did, why didn't you pick something else for me? Did you know that there would be times when I would attempt suicide? Did you? I'm angry! If you knew, why did you give me this? There's no way this was a fair choice! God, I spent over half of my life trying to figure out who I was and you could have changed this. I was forced to live a lie and pretend to be someone that I wasn't ... and for what? To be accepted by people who wouldn't like me anyway.

I still remember the feel of his hands on my penis as he told me to be quiet. I remember the look on his face as I felt sheer terror. I'll always have the impression of the scene of the night I put my finger in there ... the smell of the lotion he told me to use. I remember feeling abandoned. I still remember hoping that you would snap him into reality, but you didn't. To this day, I still get sick to my stomach when I smell that fragrance. I remember having to pretend that he was my spiritual father, when he was my lover. Why was that my THIS? Wasn't I good enough to protect? Wasn't I worth saving?

How could I tell people that I was... You know what it is. How could I hide my affection? How could I cover it up? Would the people who loved me see me differently? Would my sexuality matter? If I liked men would that make me bad? I didn't know any better. What do I do? I don't want to be THIS, but I still find myself living THIS. I'm confused. Help me get out of this!

Signed,

~ A Child Who's Angry about the Cards He Was Dealt

YOU DIDN'T LET ME SEE THIS ONE

Dear Sovereign,

I was right there. I was walking back from the store just two blocks over. Two blocks! I saw the traffic piled up almost some ten blocks backwards from where everyone was trying to get. I made light of traffic and all the poor souls who had to sit there until every car inched its way down the long, winding blocks to the freeway, and I halfheartedly thanked you that it wasn't me who had to sit and wait because I am so impatient.

As the fire trucks whizzed by and the ambulance horns and bells flooded our ears, I did what my mother had always taught me to do. I said a quick prayer to send you to the scene and hoped everything would be all right. Truth be told, we were used to this on the Stockton, CA streets. We lived in a great house on a great block, but we were always so close to gang violence.

Someone somewhere around was always getting shot. We were just used to it. I always prayed for the families when the news reports would come out, always. I felt so sorry for those loved ones and could not imagine their pain. It didn't matter if they were thugs or not. The death of any loved one as a parent, sibling, cousin, or other relative was still very sad, and I wished that kind of pain on no one.

As for me, I always felt safe. It did not matter what time of day or if it was the earliest hours of the morning, I did what I wanted to do when I wanted to do it. If I wanted something as minor as ice cream at 3:00 a.m., I thought nothing at all of jumping in the car or even walking the few blocks to Winco (a local grocery store) for it.

It's funny, I can still hear my baby brother's voice when he would spot me out, especially late at night, saying, "It's not safe, Reina." I would shrug him off as usual because we were two different people. He was way more involved in street life than I was. In my arrogance I believed that if you lived by the sword you'd die by it. Internally I always told myself it was him who should be thankful that *my* prophetic eyes and diligence in prayer were keeping *him* safe.

I mean I did have evidence. There was no lie in that thought. I warned him constantly of potential threats and dangers that you showed me and relished in your consistency of helping him dodge it all. It was just our normal. We were exempt from *those* kinds of issues according to Psalm 91. We had this. It was other families that should be worried, not us. In fact, I wondered often how unlucky they might be if my family didn't live in the neighborhood. I walked those streets giving prayer my all, laying hands on houses, and declaring territorial demons down and out. We were good. There was a prophet in the city, and the God I served let me *see* it before anyone had a chance to see it materialize.

So imagine my surprise when, hours after I walked back from Walmart, detectives were showing up at our door to declare to my mother that her son had been shot and killed. All I could do was hold my chest and scream. Did you feel it? Did you feel my shortness of breath and the shooting pains from my chest to my head? Were you aware that the blood was rushing so fast to my brain that I couldn't even stand? I can still hear my dog barking in the yard trying to get to me. I still remember the way the pain engulfed me.

Never in my life have I ever felt so let down. My brother had done nothing but befriend the wrong man who had an order to kill him because of something he accidentally saw. How is this fair for a holy house? God, I was right there. I was just one block over. How is it you gave me every warning and every instinct concerning him all those years but left out this one moment? You didn't let me *see*.

I spent two years ministering and living in a depressed state. I still kept going because he would have wanted me to, but the pain that attached itself when we got the news has never left the center of my chest. Was I off? Has everything been a lie? I feel so insecure and unsure now. How does this happen to a believing household with a resident prophet? These tears burn relentlessly at the thought. I'm tired of eyes filled with tears. I need to understand where Psalm 91 failed me—where our relationship stopped producing the rearguard you promised me. How can I minister after this when my prayers clearly aren't as effective as I assumed and my sight is not as sharp as I thought?

If I could have just held his hand... Why didn't you let me see? I was one ... block ... over! I could have prayed. I could have travelled with him in the ambulance. I could have laid my hands and watched his recovery. I don't know for sure, I just feel like I could have done *something*. I feel like a fraud. This is too much. I don't want to hear it is going to be okay. Nothing about this has been okay. Almost three years sitting in and out of courtrooms at my brother's murder trial—words I thought would never apply to my family—has given me an internal disdain for faith.

It is not that I don't love you. You know my heart and all its inner workings. I just feel like a fraud. I am not sure how I can stand up and declare your goodness when my heart feels so forsaken and dare I say betrayed. My baby brother is DEAD. Just like that—gone. I failed him. If there is some magic strategy for dealing with all these feelings, if there is a glimpse of any hope, I need it now. I have had dreams of my interlocked fingers around the throat of anyone else who tells me you know best. I am drowning in sorrow—walking under water from pulpit to pew to home and through life. My confidence is shaken. My faith has taken a hit. The fabric of everything I believed has come undone. *I am undone.*

I don't want to be a prophetic fraud. I want to believe again. I want to feel safe again. I want to breathe normally again. I want to believe in Psalm 91. I want to know that my safety net in you is not attached by a thin thread that could break at any moment. I don't feel anything lately but numb, and as staggering as all this I am still turning to you. How is that for irony in this love faith, hate faith dynamic? I want to feel faith-normal again. I want to believe what I preach. I want to understand what probably can never be understood. Help me. My world is shaken.

Signed,

~ Your Daughter Who Feels Abandoned

THE PURPOSE OF PAIN

You will know the depth of my love through the extent of your suffering. What you see as harsh I say is light. What you say is hard, I say is graced. The measure of my love is endless, for I am the God of unsearchable, inexhaustible boundaries. I avail myself to my children when they are in need. I desire that you would know me. I will never hide myself from you.

I cannot show you my face, but I can overwhelm you with my love and my presence. My love is displayed through my goodness. I am the type of father that takes care of his children. I said that my goodness and my mercy would follow you eternally. Have I not proven that to be true? Have I not shown you the height and depth of my love as your Father?

I choose to receive you with love that is everlasting. My love stretches beyond the shores of the ocean and beyond the peaks of the mountain. My love will capture you in every space that you find yourself in. From this day forward, you will become acquainted with the nature of a father. You'll be able to discern what is ordained by me. Reject anything that does not match my nature in likeness of care.

Change your perspective about the plight of your suffering. All that you have lived through, I use to get my glory. Your life is a testament to my ability to form a masterpiece from clay pieces that others would count as trash. So this day I proclaim that you are not the result of your life story. There is more that has yet to be unearthed. Consider that your life was orchestrated to reveal immense potential and capacity. Consider that aspects of your personhood would not carry meaning had they not been revealed through fire. My fire purifies but also ignites passion within.

I amplify pain to reveal purpose. Purpose is like a diamond buried beneath the shore. This diamond is fashioned through contact with fire and pressure. It must stay hidden until the earth's elements have completed their creative processes, so as not to compromise the brilliance or value of the diamond. It is delivered to the surface when creation knows that it is safe to handle. This diamond must be buffed so that its radiance can never be diminished. The value of the diamond increases with each striation it receives.

Such is the same with you. You've felt that life was a series of unjust happenings. Yet, you had no idea what was being discovered within you. So count this as a moment of instruction. Now you've become acquainted with the ingenuity that is needed to master the war for your future. Your sins are not worth mentioning anymore; I have already forgiven them and thrown them far from me. They will not count against you.

So never again will you say that you are helpless. Never again will you say that you are full of despair. You will strike the language of the broken from your lips. You will strike the language of the helpless from your lips. "Woe is me" will never be your portion. You will, instead, rely upon the strength that lives within. For this day comes out of you a valiant warrior that is not acquainted with those that are orphaned. This day I say be free to live.

You were never an orphan. You were adopted into my family before you entered the earth. You were designed as a purpose before you were a person. Now you have met your person and your purpose.

~ God

RELENTLESS LOVE

My Child,

I have earned the right to a parental claim, and I must be parental with you now. You should first understand that I am not insensitive to your pain or ignorant to your plight. I Am that I Am. You know that in that alone is more power and wisdom than you can ascertain. You cannot contain all of me; however, that does not mean that I am not close to the brokenhearted (Psalm 34:18).

I know grief. I know my every desire for you and for nations and generations nailed to a cross and the pain of choosing to let it be so, so that you could draw close to me. Yes, I know pain and feeling forsaken over and over again by my own creation. I am the Absolver and the Resolver moving through time and generation—the preeminent God who *is* the answer before the questions exist—yet still and always so willing to receive every care you cast on me.

I am not deterred by your feelings and how they sometimes impact your faith. I gave you the ability to feel as a means of connection with me, while I work in the facts. The fact is I owe no one anything, but I extend myself nonetheless. You could never understand what I do and why I do it. I know the answers you are seeking. You want to understand why some die and some don't. You want to understand why for some a plane crash and others a peaceful night's sleep transition. You wonder if you can really trust me or if I am some cruel, unjust God who has made you all pawns in a civil (Kingdom) war. These are questions that finite understanding cannot hold, but what if I changed the question?

Have I ever been unfaithful or absent of good? Have my wings ever failed as a shield? Am I not enough? Your grief is real. You want answers that soothe your logic and reason, but I am Reason. I am Peace. I am Hope. I am the reverse of every curse. In your pain you perceive the promise has failed. You perceive the scriptures to have been rendered powerless as declaration, but they were never written to bear the weight of human rationale. They have always been a resource and a guide to me—insight into who I am and a higher wisdom you must free-fall in me to find. Psalm 91 didn't fail. It has been working for you from the day I planted you in the womb, and it did not fail your brother.

Every relationship I have is individual. Every conversation I have is an individual one. Every plan I have for you lives in my hands, it is between you and me. You may be indirectly affected, but it didn't happen to you. It happened to him. You see it as a life gone too soon; I see it as one that accomplished what I set forth for it to do. You see murder as vile and cruel, and indeed it is. His path was set. Your brother was called to people that people like you would never otherwise touch. The lives he impacted were lives that were never going to approach a church entrance. There are worlds outside of the walls of a building that need me just as much as you do.

Those worlds are dark and hold their own consequences. I know the lights I put in those places for a greater purpose to demonstrate and reveal my love *and* my judgment. My agents come in all forms in every area of life at every level of life. That will not always look like you desire. Psalm 91 covered him until his assignment was finished. Death is still defeated. No matter how death enters, my rest is victory. My "finished" will not go beyond what I set to do through them because they will be sorely missed. Some of my agents will never minister in a pulpit or cast out demons, but they are lights just the same. That is where you have to trust my character. This is why your every process begins with an extension of my character to you and then in you, and finally through you, so that you will know that, no matter what, I AM. I use murder too. I prove myself in every cancer, in every ailment, and in every pain.

I was with you when you went to Walmart, which is why I didn't show you. I knew what you could handle and I knew what was still lurking in the area. I am the same God that covered you from every rapist, thief, and drive-by as you walked fearlessly to Winco. I redirected gang bangers and sex traffickers because I knew you'd be walking down that street at a set time. I cannot fail.

Your brother needed me as he lay there without interruption. We had a conversation there that drew him into me. He made peace with death and entered into my rest. It was beautiful. Through this I have not decreased but increased in you. I did not order his hit, but I am still using it as **you** live and carry his memory and eventually minister to others who will face similar pain. Life is not easy. It holds dark things that may appear to win on the surface, but no matter what dark forces introduce, I have never lost ONE that belonged to me. Human life can be taken. A soul returned to me has earned its reward.

~ God

FORGIVENESS IS OVERRATED

Dear God,

Forgiveness is overrated. I know, I know; 70 x 7 (Matthew 18:22) and forgive if I want to be forgiven (Matthew 6:14–15). It's a high idea that I used to think I understood. In theory it doesn't seem that difficult. It's downright noble if you ask me. But having to sit in a courtroom and look my brother's killer in the face and say, "I forgive you," is downright asinine. I want to see him fry. I want to see him and every accomplice he had lose their life for taking one that was so important and so special to me.

And don't get me started on my grandmother. God rest her soul, but her life meant death to mine—death to my emotional health and self-esteem. She hated me and she showed it by prostituting me as a toddler, beating me mercilessly, torturing me with two large dogs, and let's not forget the all-day "reasons why she hated my existence" speeches. What grandmother treats their grandchild that way? And why did she get to pass away so calmly without ever having to pay for any of it? I never got to flaunt my success in her face or show her who I had become In the face of her hate. I wanted her to see me and regret every foul thing she ever said to me! I deserved that!

And then there is the only father I knew ... once my hero

turned drug addicted and molester/rapist. I don't mean to say that so cruelly. We all have our issues. Drugs brought the worst of darkness out in him. Still, I was phenomenally affected, and the next time I would see him alive he was so out of it he could barely remember my name.

Why is this the story of my life? Why do people get to keep doing horrible things to me and then get to go on and live fruitful lives like nothing ever happened? They show no kindness or remorse. They are not ignorant to how they hurt and abused me, and they have the audacity to call themselves your children. Where is my recompense? Where is my support? Why is it I can so easily take responsibility for my part in situations? I can be mature enough to apologize, but I never get that back in return.

Signed,

~ Bitter

UNWANTED ANGER

Dear God,

I need your help! I am so tired of hurting people. I am 22 years old. I have five kids and I am not with any of their mothers. All my friends have kids too. My mom raised me on her own and did the best she could. I know you know while she was working, I was out in the streets; even though I wasn't supposed to be. I know it's my fault and I'm sorry. It started out as a game with my friends, trying to see how many women we could get. But now everything is out of control! I know how serious it is to raise children, but I really don't know how. My kids didn't ask to be here. I want to do better, but I don't know how! I don't know how! I am here asking you for help. I don't have any real skills for a job, and the only thing I know is the streets. I can't keep hanging with my friends. I know I need to grow up and be a man, but I just don't know what that looks like. I need your help, please.

My father left when I was five and all I remember of him was him being put in handcuffs and placed in the back of the cop car after beating my mother. So, I have never had a role model to teach me how to be a father. I heard he got out of jail, but I don't even know where he is. My grandma said you can change my name and make me new. I would really like that. So please give me a chance. I want to do right by my kids and show them a better life. So, if you could please help me, I will be very grateful.

P.S. Can you also help me get rid of my anger too? I think that would really help.

Signed,

~ The Pissed Off One

ABANDONMENT ISSUES

Dear God,

From a young age, you knew I was fatherless and of the half stories I was told about the abusive father who abandoned me. I really didn't know I was missing anything until lately because I had my mother and she was all I needed; at least that's what I believed. But she is gone now and so are most of the men that have been in my life. So can we talk about the abandonment issues I have, about the feelings of not being enough, the feelings of rejection, and, oh yeah, can we also talk about why you allowed all this to happen? Was it really necessary to go through all of this? Will it ever end or do I have to wait for the sweet by and by? I really need to know because I don't want to be alone. I want to trust again, but I don't know how. So I was wondering if you would like to be my father since I don't have one? I really believe you would be a good father for me. The perfect father and a perfect place to start trusting. Being fatherless I believe has something to do with all these issues I have, but I am not sure. I believe you would be a good father, but I haven't made very good choices lately and I am not sure this is going to be a good one either. If you promise not to leave me, I promise to try not to push you away. I promise to be the best daughter ever.

Love,

~ Your daughter-in-waiting,

COME BACK HOME

Dear Son / Daughter,

It's been a while since we last spoke. Where have you been? I've missed you. We used to speak daily and now it's been about two months since our last conversation. Tell me what's new in your life. What decisions have you made without me? I miss you! I want to be involved in your life. I feel like you shut me out. I know you got confused and felt like I left you, but I'm still here. I have always been. There was a time when trouble used to push you closer to me, now it seems to drive you away from me. Where did you go?

What or who took you away from me? Where have you been? Have you found another god? What has gotten you distracted? Where did you go? Did I do something to push you away? Was it something I said or did that made you leave? I just want the chance to make it right. There was a time when you'd talk to me about everything, now I can't seem to find you. I miss you.

I sent my servants to remind you that I was waiting for you. I even sent a few dreams your way. I thought those would lead you back to me, but they didn't. Where did we go wrong? Did someone else get in the way? What did they have that I didn't? What did they offer that I didn't or couldn't? I know life was hard, but we conquered many things together. Just talk to me. We can work it out.

I'm leaving this letter hoping that you'll see it. I put it in the place where we would always meet. I'll leave it here for you to see when you return. I'll check in to see if you came back to me. I'll be waiting for you. I love you, son / daughter.

Signed,

~ A Broken-Hearted Father (GOD)

SOMETIMES "IN" IS THE "OUT"

My Child,

You are looking for the way out when you should be looking for the way in. I am not unaware of the things that you have faced, nor did I authorize them. I am the giver of good not evil. Evil comes from only one place. In life you will be a victim of the choices people around you make, and you will make choices that victimize other people. That is what it is to live in the flesh in an inherently evil world—a world forfeited by decisions made back in the garden. Issues began in a garden and were redeemed in one.

That redemption has not escaped you. Every struggle you face is an exposure of something inside of you that needs liberty. You want to see yourself as good, and my creations are in fact good, but the fact remains that, yes, evil is always present. The strategies for overcoming evil are available to you if you truly desire them. The same intense vigor that led you to pornographic media content and to open your legs in houses and hotel rooms, and even abortion clinics, is the same vigor you need when approaching the Throne of Grace. You need not be ashamed or embarrassed. Your struggles aren't new or new to me.

Do you know why the command to be transformed by the renewing of your mind exists (Romans 12:1-2)? It is because

I knew that life would shape your choices and decisions. I knew that darkness would try to snuff out every light. I issued this as a warning that your present mind is not your final mind and you should seek something higher.

Breaking the power of curses and addictions, habits and soul ties does not happen by your own strength. Too often my children fail at the work of worship that leads them to a breakthrough. They choose to suffer in silence because of shame and condemnation I have not placed on them. Suffering does not groom heroes, deliverance does. You must want that deliverance as badly as you want love.

One reason you keep finding yourself in this cycle is because deep down you want to prove your value. I have watched you reject well-meaning people from your life in favor of those who bring toxicity and more abuse because you need to resolve the past (even if you don't understand that is what you are doing). The enemy has perverted your thinking and your assessment of life and yourself. I want to change that thinking and expose you to truth—my truth.

If you believe the "out" to all of this is found in marriage, sex, or whatever gratification you feel you need, you will resign yourself to a cycle. You may even find some good, but that will always be far less than my good, which has far greater implications for the present and future than you know. I need to teach you how to see yourself the way I see you.

When I tell you the way out is in, I am telling you to come closer—to fall into me. To do the opposite is to keep falling into the same traps. I am less concerned with what you do and more concerned with helping you understand why you do it so we can break it *together*. It is in our intimate time that I show you where I was when you needed me most.

It saddens me when you deeply sigh and treat prayer like it

is an ineffective chore. Time with me is powerful, it provides healing, answers, and strategies. How you approach me determines how you experience me. I am a Rewarder of those that diligently seek me (Hebrews 11:6). The reward *is* me. The reward is revelation about who you are and where you are headed and why you have faced what you have. Do not let your attitude render me powerless or helpless. Do not insult my authority with your unwilling energy. I am that I am, and I have a plan for your life that supersedes any personal issue.

Deliverance is not always in the form of a release from a desire. Sometimes the release is *of you* to the mountain I have assigned to you. When your desire for me supersedes your flesh, your flesh can then bow to me. Self-control is obtained through worship. When I am your highest priority, so much that has held you hostage will release you. Give me that same energy and time you put into a new love interest—the way you forego sleep to talk to them or make yourself available as often as they ask.

If you really want me, show me. If you really want to be free don't just say it, run to it relentlessly. Anyone who has ever truly relentlessly pursued me will tell you it has never failed to be worth the work. Anyone who turns his or her nose up at the idea of waiting, seeking and praying has never really known me. The choice is yours. Will you draw close or continue to be tormented by the things you can't break? Will you resign yourself to a bleak future or come after the blueprint I have already designed? Everything concerning you rests on a decision to seek or sit. You need me. I am not getting any older, but you are.

~ God

TRUST ME

This whole journey is about teaching you to trust me. To trust me means that you love me enough to not be moved when I make a move, especially one that defies the logic of your limited thinking. If I am your God, then you must give me space to make necessary adjustments as I see fit. Let your posture not change but find yourself being more resolved than ever before.

Trust my wisdom and my plan. Trust that I have your world in my hands. Trust that I am the only one that can write the narrative for your life. Trust that my will far exceeds any and every thought you could have. Trust that I am full of compassion and will never let you escape the grips of my love. Trust that I am your present help.

Regard mercy and truth in high honor.

Many people don't love me. They want me according to their terms. That is not how I have designed a relationship to work. It's a matter of mutual exchange and harmony. My desire for you is that you would love me fully. Love me with no measure and no boundaries.

This is the moment to push away the distractions. Dethrone and disregard anything that could draw you away from me.

Shun anything that could change your perception of me. I am a jealous God. I will not change. There is no variance found within me.

I want to have a relationship with you, as I have longed for your return to me. I want to commune with you and show you things that you do not know. I want to be the only source of provision that you need. I want to be the place of your peace, but you must allow me to have unhindered fellowship with you.

Hide my truth in your heart.

You will no longer regard yourself as an orphan. As you decide to trust me, you will yield to me. As you yield to me, the barriers that hide your broken heart will be opened. As you give me your heart, you will learn that I am full of love. I desire to shower you with this love as we journey together into your next.

Will you allow me to love you? Will you allow me to give you joy? This joy does more than make you smile. It gives you reasons to try again. My joy gives you courage to stand boldly in the face of difficulty, knowing that I go before you to ensure that you are triumphant. As you trust me you'll learn that there cannot be failure with me.

Acknowledge that I am.

Allow me to lead you. The greatest dilemma you will face is the continual need to maintain control. Sonship is a matter of being taught through instruction. Trust that I am a wise instructor and the words that I share will lead to life. A restoration of life. You cannot carry this weight on your own. Therefore, yield to my leading and harbor my instruction. I will lead you into paths uncharted, but not paths that are deadly. This moment is about reconstructing your life. You can only do that with and through me, as all life is found in me.

Don't harden your heart towards me. Trust me. Start this journey by giving me control of the small things. Allow me to show you that I am who I say I am. I am not like fragile humans. My words convey the thoughts of my heart.

My child, trust that I know what is best for you. I know what path you should take, and which you should avoid. Trust my direction. Free yourself from this constant need for validation. You are my beloved, is that not validation enough? Do not look to man for that which you can only find with me. You have no need to seek another for approval of how I've created you. You are my chosen. My beloved. You are mine!

~ Your Father

I BELONG TO YOU

I don't know where to start, so I'll just share what's on my heart.

I'm struggling with this thought that you love me unconditionally. I've confessed that you are Lord and Savior, or at least that's what they told me to do. I don't doubt that you are real, but I struggle to accept the thought that you can love me – a sinner – without boundary or limitation. They say we have to believe that you are near to the brokenhearted, and you love sinners the same as saints. How can this be? You're perfect. I'm... flawed. HOW can we exist as a 'family' if I look nothing like you? I'm not trying to limit what you can do. Am I overthinking this God, I'm sorry if I've offended you.

It took a great deal of courage to even admit that much.

I've tried to conquer my sins and live upright, but it's difficult. I'm faced with a decision each day to live for you or to live for me. I want to do both, but I know I can't be loyal to you and another and say that I love you only. My sin nature gets the best of me. It's part of me. It's so easy and tempting to live reckless. This culture that I live in makes it EASY to give into temptation.

God, I feel like I'm a failure. I've tried to change many times and it always ends in ruin. I want something different for my life. I've heard so much about you. I want to know you. Will you receive me, knowing everything I've done wrong? I can admit that I've failed. Honestly, some days I haven't tried as much as I should have. Is there any way of being redeemed from that? I honestly don't know what to do at this point. Suicide isn't an option, but if I could find a way to escape ME, I would.

I feel like there's no fix for me because I'm *different*.

They said, "Go to church, it'll make you feel better." I tried that, and it failed. Church made everything worse actually. "Be consistent. Come to Bible study," they said. I went, but that didn't discipline my temptation. "Be accountable to people." That was a great idea, but the liar in me found ways to paint a picture of success when there was nothing but disaster.

I read in your Word that everything connected to me is made perfect when you're involved. It's clear that you're the only person who can fix this mess in my life. Then I read that your love is perfect and without restriction and it even casts away fear. Am I fearful or extremely anxious?

Can your love cast away all of my fear? Is it possible to be anxious for nothing? How does that happen? Everything around me looks like death. This has become my norm. How do I find life when everything around me looks like death? I don't know how I would feel if things were different. My life reflects despair currently, a despair that is so real to me.

God, please deal with this fear that drives me to deny the

truth. Deal with my fear that I'll simply wander aimlessly until I disappear one day. Deal with this fear of not finding the place where I belong. Deal with this fear that I'll never feel complete.

Signed,

~ Displaced and Different

I'M GRATEFUL

Dear God,

I'm writing this letter today to express something I haven't said to you in a while—THANK YOU! Life has been... Wow, where do I begin? It's been hard, but I'm still alive. I don't take enough time to smell the roses. I haven't been grateful for what you've done. I recognize that you're good, but I don't always stop to tell you. I don't appreciate you as much as I should. I've been so consumed with all the things in my life that I haven't stopped to just be ... grateful.

I have a list of things to be grateful for. I'm alive. I'm healthy. I'm able to move and think for myself. Things aren't nearly as bad as they sometimes seem to be. I woke up today and I feel better than I do most days. I don't have a reason to complain. Yes, things could be better; but they could also be worse. I could make a list of things to be upset about, but I won't. Today, I choose to be grateful.

Lord, I thank you for your love and your grace. I thank you for the life you've given me and all that I have. I thank you for the blessings that I've been given, even the ones I have overlooked. appreciate your thoughtfulness and love for me. I am in awe of your goodness. In a world full of madness, darkness and chaos you are consistently peace, light and sanity. You keep me grounded when I feel like my life is floating in a million directions.

Today, and every day, I will be intentional about taking time to reflect on your goodness. I will be intentional about praising you and putting things back into perspective. Thank you, Lord, for being good!

Signed,

~ A Child Who Is Grateful

DADDY DEAREST

My Dearest Daddy,

I have made up my mind that I am going to wait on you this time. I promise I will not get ahead of you. I am going to sit right here and wait for the promise you gave me. I am not going to ask you for more patience. I am going to work with the amount you already gave me. I know I can do it with your help. Remember the last time I didn't listen? I found myself walking down the highway at night. I was afraid someone was going to run me over or kidnap me. All because I didn't listen to you. Oh! Remember the time you told me to stay home and eat with my family? I just had to go and eat with my friends. I got so sick. Man! I never want to experience that again! Food poisoning is no joke. How about the time you told me not to marry you know who? I don't even want to mention his name. As usual I went ahead and did it anyway. I sure wish I would have listened. It took you to get me out of that one.

Why don't I listen? It seems like I always have to learn the hard way. Like the time when you told me you were going to give me a car. I was so excited. So, what did I do? I went out and bought a new car. But you said you were going to buy me one not that I was going to buy it. That car didn't even last a whole year. I had so much trouble with that car. You didn't even hold it against me and, just like you said, you gave me a new car. I didn't even have to pay for it. If I would have listened to you, I wouldn't have wasted all that money. Wow! As I am talking, I am realizing that I haven't been listening well at all. I am so sorry. I will do better. Please forgive me.

Sincerely,

~ Your Daughter who thinks she knows everything

I'M HOLDING ON TO YOU

My Son,

Many have fallen, but I will not let you fall. I will uphold you with my right hand. I know times may seem hard and uncertain with death lingering all around, but nothing and no one determines when death will come except me. Death and life are in the power of my hands. So, know you will not see death until your purpose is done. Settle yourself. No longer will you walk in fear. I am empowering you to walk in boldness and strength. In my name you will go forth. So, don't look to the right, don't look to the left, and don't look behind you. Look straight ahead and go forth and in the power of my might.

Signed,

~ Your Heavenly Father

NO LONGER SLAVES

My child, do you believe that I am sovereign, meaning I am he that makes no mistake? There is no error to my wisdom, for my thoughts and my desires toward you far exceed anything you could desire of yourself. I am the God of miracles. My desire is to endow you with great power that produces miracles, but I must qualify you according to the measure of grace given you. My child, this breaking isn't to crush you. This breaking is to prove YOU worthy before the world.

As my Word declares, I formed you before the earth was founded. I have already outlined the course of your days. I have predestined you to carry the fullness of my glory and to manifest the living Christ for all to see. Therefore, despise not my chastening. Shun not the journey to prepare you. For many have said before, "Lord, I'll go," but have failed to successfully carry this mandate. For many have said before, "Lord, use me," but have neglected to come right before me. My child, my desire is to amplify the reach of your voice. For there are places and people that I have afore-destined for you to reach. I trust you to carry my name as your banner. I trust that you will not desecrate the sanctity of my name.

My desire is to set you as a watchman over the heavens and the earth. For the day of new dawning is upon you, and I shall glorify myself through you. For these are the days of great glory. For my glory will encompass you as you journey about fulfilling my will.

Even as Aaron was given a staff, I will give you that same power in your hands. I will give you how to discern and rule righteously. For you are one that I have chosen to endow with an everlasting love. Yea, even I shall give you a measure of my heart that will draw mankind to you and to me. You will not rule like those before you that made me appear as a tyrant. Yes, I am a jealous God, but my jealousy does not end in anger, except you rob me of what is mine.

Even as the sons of Issachar were anointed to discern the times and seasons, I shall be, with you, a compass that leads you into the paths ahead. As I was with my Son, so shall I be with you. Go forth, my child, into the days that are ahead. Have no fear for I will roar from within you. I have already conquered the mountain that stands before you. My charge to you is to ascend and reclaim for my name. Do this and it shall be to you and the peoples of the earth a spring in the desert. It shall be a sign of the coming hope that returns to the earth.

Know that my love is the place of your retreat. My love becomes a place of refuge for the wounded soul. Find your peace in me and the anxieties of yesteryear, you will see no more. All has led to this moment, and now I say to you that I love you. I am the Father that will never present you ill-prepared or lacking for anything.

Do you remember those times when I would overwhelm you with my presence? I would remind you of the times you met my goodness? It has all been to prove to you that I am fairest of them all. So, yes, the unfolding of my will has seemed harsh, but I have increased your capacity and taught you what it means to make your dwelling in me.

Go forth, and know that I delight in you.

~ God

I AM YOUR SANCTUARY

My Child,

The psalmist expressed this same feeling in Psalm 73, but that expression did not end in pain. By verse 17 the writer had a revelation—sanctuary! I offer sanctuary to you today.

When I reached for you from outside of time, to place you in the earth, on a mountain for such a time as this, I could not and did not promise you that darkness would not at least try to overtake you. The light of you drew his evil eye, but I have always responded to his every attack against you. You were not defeated then, and you are not defeated now. Life is only as tragic as you speak it to be.

I have never been a sadistic God who has taken delight in your pain for my personal glory. I have, however, been a God who has taken your pain and turned it into purpose. I have earned the right to require you to forgive. You must understand, though, that forgiveness is for you. If I am adamant about it, even in the worst of circumstances, it is because your adversary knows well how to feed on these things and turn a pure heart bitter and enraged. An enraged heart slew his brother (Genesis 4). An enraged heart stole a birthright (Genesis 25:19–34). An enraged heart would not let my people go (Exodus 5). What an enraged heart does merits consequences. I will never allow you to be used as a pawn in an evil game.

I am not asking you to forget. I am asking you to fall into me so that you will have nothing in common with him (John 14:30). When I ask you to forgive, as painful and unfair as it may seem, I am truly saving you, more than you know, over and over again. It's not a punishment. Forgiveness is a prize. It carries with it destiny and power. Do not let emotions make you underestimate it.

~ God

YOUR CORONATION

Arise! Come before me. I want to crown you. You have been found to be faithful in the things that I have given you. You have followed me with your whole heart and have not given into the things of this world. A great harvest of souls is coming, and I have chosen you for the work. Don't worry, you are not alone. There are others that I am sending forth not many days from now. You will have a visitation where you will be given a set of instructions. If you follow them and do not detour from what I am calling you to do, you and your family and generations to come shall be saved.

Signed,

~ The God of Promotion

ENTER IN

I the Lord your God love you and want to use you for my glory; for this reason I have not allowed you to destroy yourself. I have extended grace, mercy, and my love since the beginning. I have been waiting to call you into sonship instead of servant hood. I have been calling you into a place of intimacy to tell you the plans and the strategies that I have for you to walk into your destiny. Yet, you continue to reject me and walk in your own way. You continue to do things your way and by your own might. You have been seeing through the eyes of your own understanding. And because of it, you have been frustrated, angry, and confused wondering why things don't look the way you feel they should. I want to remind you of the promises I made to you that you have forgotten. Look to me. Call me and I will answer. You have made your own plans, but, today, if you surrender to me, I will empower you to go forth. I will protect you, provide for you, and give you peace. Everything you need is in me. Enter into my rest.

Signed,

~ The God of Promise

FOREVER TO LOVE YOU

My Child,

Who else loves you enough to leave the beauty and splendor of Heaven to come to Earth, to die. I died for You! I came to die so that I could leave to wait for you in eternity. It's the greatest love ever told. The things I have for you will not be able to be contained in the flesh. The colors, the fragrances, the visions, and my Presence! All a feast for all the senses known and unknown for you. I will lavish on you a new reality. I plan to love you forever. You are my prize, my beloved, my favorite one. How fair you are, my love, my bride. My promise of love will not end in affairs, divorce, or heartbreak. I've vowed to covenant with you before you knew of me. I spilled my blood that you would never taste of death. My love is stronger than death. You should have no fear for I've covered you in the safety of my tower. You are no damsel in distress for I've destroyed every enemy of my Kingdom. Your garments are made of the finest fabrics, your ring a pure stone with no blemish, your chambers await your rest. You are a queen worthy of her crown! Your position is sure!

Forever Your Love,

~ God

AFFIRMED BY ABBA

Dear Son / Daughter,

I know what they have said to you. I know they damaged you. I know they hurt you; but I want to affirm you! You are more than what they tried to make you think you were not! You may not have heard these things enough, so I want you to hear them now. Let the whispers and even loud, bold declarations of my love cover you and pull you up!

You are enough!

You are strong!

You are the apple of my eye!

I love you!

I'm proud of you!

You will be successful!

You are destined for greatness!

You don't have to settle for that!

You have more in you than you know!

You are special! A rare find!

You are my special pick! My chosen one!

I love you!

I will never leave you!

You are a part of my plan!

It's okay to be afraid!

It's okay to not be okay!

It's okay to not know what to do!

You don't have to have it all figured out! The beauty of life is sometimes found in moments of failure!

YOU ARE MY BELOVED CHILD!

~ God,

Your Loving & Proud Father

Psalm 139:14 (NKJV) – "I will praise you, for I am fearfully and wonderfully made; marvelous are your works, and that my soul knows very well."

> 1 Peter 2:9 (NKJV) – "But you are a chosen generation, a royal priesthood, a holy nation, His own special people, that you may proclaim the praises of Him who called you out of darkness into His marvelous light."

About the Authors

About the Authors

LATRICE LEAKE

Is a prophetic voice for this end-time generation. She is transparent, organic, and authentic. Latrice has received prophetic training under the leadership of Apostle Tom and Prophet Phyllis Ryneckie at Sapphire Family Church under the covering of Prophet, Bishop Dr. Bill Hammond, founder of Christian International Ministries. She was later consecrated as a prophet of the Lord in May of 2010. She served under the leadership of Pastor Shawn L. Bell and First Lady Faye Bell and was trained and further equipped for the work of ministry. The Lord has placed her carefully under her pastors, Dr. Jonathan Patterson and Pastor Raequel Patterson, at

The Lord's Harvest Church in Baltimore, MD.

In 2012, she published her first book, ***Prophetic Waters for the Thirsty Soul***. In 2014, she birthed out Kingdom Kulture Ministries, 3 Fold Cord Ministries, and The Heal Our Men movement along with The Help Wives and Wives-in-Waiting series. She can be found hosting initiatives to feed the homeless and promote women's empowerment and events that edify the body of Christ. Prophetess Leake hosts weekly prophetic prayer calls and enjoys pouring into the lives of God's people. She currently hosts The School of the Prophetic to train and activate prophets and those who flow in prophetic ministry.

Prophetess Leake's desire to see the works of the Lord made manifest in His people is the driving force that has propelled His handmaiden into action though her spiritual walk with Him. Walking in the Office of the Prophet and heavily in intercession allows her to pray with eagle-like precision for the servants of the Lord and to uplift the weakest of men. This passionate worshiper, innovative facilitator, and intercessor ministers to the building of God's church and desires to see the captive set free and loosed from the yoke and bondage of sin and shame.

With an ear to the mouth and pulse of God, Latrice Leake is releasing an end-time word and putting her hands to the plow in the Kingdom of God. Her desire is to turn the hearts of men back to their God through teaching, preaching, and prophecy. She is reclaiming territory in Jesus' name by decreeing, declaring, and demanding that the altars of this world shall be the altars of our God. Her unique style and approach to delivering the word of God is fresh, exciting, and for the glory of the Father alone. We look forward to working the works of the Father with you and building His

Kingdom one heart at a time! Jeremiah 29:11 "For I know the plans I have for you," declares the Lord, "plans to prosper you and not to harm you, plans to give you hope and a future."

Contact us through email
Prophetessleake@gmail.com

or

visit our website www.LatriceLeake.com

JUSTIN RUFFIN

PROPHET JUSTIN RUFFIN is a highly anointed and skilled gift to the body of Christ. He was born in Clinton, Maryland, and was raised to fear the Lord by his grandmother, Minister Helen Young, and other members of his family. He accepted the Lord in his life at the early age of six and has grown greatly in the Lord since that time. He is a product of the Prince George's County School District, where he graduated from Eleanor Roosevelt High School with his diploma. In 2016, he received his A.A. degree in Early Childhood Education and is presently pursuing his B.A. in Organizational Leadership.

Prophet Ruffin has been in ministry for more than 15 years, during which time he has traveled throughout the United States preaching, teaching, and declaring the word of God.

His unique presentation of the gospel has enabled him to minister to people of many denominations and organizations. As a result, he is a much sought-after preacher, teacher, prophet, leader, and counselor. Moreover, his gift has made room for him, allowing him to minister to his spiritual leaders, co-laborers, colleagues, family, and friends. Additionally, he has counseled many children and adults regarding life and ministry.

Prophet Ruffin is a prophet called by God and it has been his privilege to serve at various retreats, conferences, and seminars as a keynote speaker and panelist. Prophet Ruffin lives by Luke 12:47-48 (MSG): "The servant who knows what his master wants and ignores it, or insolently does whatever he pleases, will be thoroughly thrashed. But if he does a poor job through ignorance, he'll get off with a slap on the hand. Great gifts mean great responsibilities; greater gifts, greater responsibilities." He truly understands that much will be required of those to whom much is given.

Prophet Ruffin is an author. His first book, **"Anchored: A Journey to Balance, Stability & Wholeness"**, was released in 2017. As a result of its release, many doors have been opened for Prophet Ruffin and many lives have been impacted. He is currently working on his second publication, which will also focus on internal healing and stability.

Prophet Ruffin has also been blessed to host several conferences. Tamar's Cry, an annual empowerment event, was first launched in 2015 and was designed to moved people from places of stagnation and into victory. The Lord has also blessed him to host "The Ascension", which is a prophetic prayer and worship gathering designed to help the body of Christ ascend to their next place in God, and Unstopping the Dams & Releasing the Rivers, which was birthed by God to help the people of God break free from the bondages of Satan and be released into the things of

God.

Prophet Ruffin is a teacher, preacher, prophet, son, grandson, brother, uncle, godfather, and friend; but most of all he is anointed by God and he knows that his first calling is to worship the Lord.

Email: JRMinistries01@gmail.com

Phone: 240-203-8611

Website: www.justinruffin.org

JUSTIN'S ACKNOWLEDGEMENTS

Father, I thank you for allowing me to release these letters to your children. You have truly proven yourself to be the Faithful Father that never fails. I want to thank my mother, Kim Vinson, grandmother, Helen Young, and aunt, Teri Burnett, for their relentless push and support. Your intentional push and presence in my life has been amazing.

To every person who will read this book and these letters, I pray that you will be strengthened, sharpened, challenged, and healed in every area of your life. I pray that my personal experience and our collective experiences that are chronicled in this book speak life to your spirit. You were on the heart and mind of God when this book was being written and you're on His mind even now. I pray that you will allow the Father to open doors and spaces of healing in your life so you can become who He's called you to be. Your life is a part of the plan of God. Be encouraged; the Father loves you and so do I.

To Prophetess Latrice Leake, thank you for spearheading this project. Your sensitivity to the spirit of God, in this has been amazing. This is a timely book and I'm honored that you asked me to be a part of this. Thank you.

To my co-authors, you all are an amazing anointed group of people. The group chats, private conversations, laughs, tears, prayers, encouragement ... this entire journey has been interesting and amazing. Thank you all so much! There is a bond that was created between us and I appreciate you all so much. I am humbled and honored to be amongst such talented and amazing individuals. Your push and tenacity in the midst of allllll the setbacks have been fantastic. Thank you! #PRODUCE!

~ Justin

KIM GREEN

A lover of God's people, a published author and mentor for young women (Heart to Heart). She is also a strategic prophetic intercessor who specializes in the 911 intercession for the saved and the unsaved. She's a midwife who partners with other ministries to help birth their vision. She is a called-out-one who was consecrated for prophetic ministry by the late Apostle Nathanial Holcomb in 2014.

In 2018, she gave birth to The Sacredness of Prayer Ministry (an online prayer wall where you can leave a prayer request and a dedicated prayer team will come into agreement with you according to God's word). She is a founding and executive team member of Sisters with a Message (SWAM), a women's group that through the Holy Spirit helps to bring healing and restoration to hurting women. Kim is also the first team member to receive a minister's license under Pastor Cherri Lewis.

Kim is a graduate of Sonship School of the First Born in Killeen, Texas, and a graduate of the University of Washington with a degree in Human Service and Human Resources. Her prophetic training was under the late Apostle Nathanial Holcomb, (Mom) Minister Patricia Torres, Prophetess Latrice Leak and Prophet Justin Ruffin. Born in the state of California, she now resides in Texas with her husband Anthony and is the proud mother of five children.

Her sincere desire is to impart words of life and restoration into the lives of everyone she meets because God reconciled and restored her life back to Him. "All I had to do was exchange a life of emotional abuse and self-destruction and allow God to live in me fully ... and this was at no cost to me," says Kim. "Now, greater is He that is in me (and in you) than he that is in the world." Proverbs 18:21 says that death and life are in the power of the tongue ... and I choose life!

You can contact Kim via email: Kgreen409@yahoo.com

Or

On Facebook "The Sacredness of Prayer"

KIM'S ACKNOWLEDGMENTS

My first acknowledgment is to my Heavenly Father who watches over me and my Lord and Savior Jesus Christ. I love you more than words can express. To my husband, Anthony L. Green, I love you. You are my greatest support; you spend countless hours editing all my projects. Thank you for hanging in there with me. To my children, Leon, Ashlee, Kerrin, Natanial, and Jayden, I love you. To Prophet Latrice and Prophet Justin, thank you for all your knowledge prayers. To my father, Ken Smith, and Ma, Najela Smith, thank you for loving me. Last but not least, to my beautiful mother who's gone on to be with the Lord, you are my greatest inspiration; thank you for introducing me to the Holy Spirit. I know you are looking down and smiling.

~ Kim

J.K VANN

PROPHET J.K. VANN has taken on the mantle of carrying the transformative message of Christ to every branch of society. He operates as a pastoral prophet with a strong grace for healing and teaching.

Prophet Vann founded The Father's Heart Foundation in April 2015. The Father's Heart Foundation is the structured organization that supports his community engagement and evangelistic efforts. His desire is to see the nations of the earth experience reform and renewal. Prophet Vann stands as a voice to the forgotten demographics of the world. This charge is similar to that of both Amos and Josiah. Jeremiah 31:3 is the driving force of his entire operation. As the scripture records, lovingkindness continues to draw us all.

His first literary work, *The Believer's Introduction to Holistic*

Healing, is set to be released in the fall of 2020. Prophet Vann is a native Kansan and descends from a legacy of impactful leaders and ministers. He serves diligently in ministry operations for Rehoboth Covenant Ministries International. RCMI is led by Apostle David and Evangelist Valerie Love of Kansas City, MO.

Prophet Vann's life work can be summed up with the phrase, "Impacting humanity, transforming society, and glorifying God all the while."

Prophet JK Vann can be reached via email, jkvannministries@gmail.com,

or

phone, 316.202.8330

J.K'S ACKNOWLEDGEMENTS:

I dedicate this work to everyone who has been displaced by life's afflictions. May you find strength to recover all. Also, I say THANK YOU to my greatest inspirations: my mother, Rachel, and my late father, Michael.

~ J.K. Vann

HEIREINA PATREI JOHNSON-WALLACE

Affectionately known as "Rein" or "Lady Rein" in art, ministry, and authorship, was born and raised in San Francisco, CA, to Elder Huey P Johnson and Evangelist Yuvetta Pryor. Prior to his passing, her father prophesied over her in the womb indicating that she would be a dynamic and anointed woman of God carrying on his legacy of high-profile ministry and profound commitment to the cause of Christ and that she would be used to bring deliverance and healing to the nations.

Rein was saved, anointed, and called to preach at the tender age of seven—a ministry prodigy often astounding those who heard her preach with her keen insight, revelation, and theological reflections on the word. Her ministry was developed in the Church of God in Christ, where she held many positions in ministry respectively, including youth and young adult leader and minister, praise and worship leader, preacher, children's ministries leader, Sunday school and Bible study teacher, church administrator, drama ministries coordinator, and praise dance ministries leader.

Called to pursue advancement in ministry, Rein was later licensed as a reverend in the A.M.E. church prior to a call to leaving it to support her pastor in launching a non-denominational ministry geared toward reaching the marginalized and oppressed. It was there that she continued her work in the ministry serving as a clergy member, minister of music, and youth and children's leader while launching out as an independent and highly sought-after inspirational artist. Her ministry in music has enabled her to minister alongside gospel greats and has afforded her numerous accolades throughout the Bay Area and beyond.

While Rein grew up fully committed to ministry in every aspect, her young life outside of the church was a devastating one that included early prostitution by her grandmother, molestation, rape, abortion, and violence. Her passion for the people of God increased, especially for those with past traumatic and abusive experiences who needed support and ministry for their deeper needs and weren't being ministered to in the church. Fully persuaded that she could be used to minister to the hurting, marginalized, and oppressed, she began to seek God for the role that she could play in encouraging and promoting healing and transformation. In 2010, God ushered her off of a lucrative job as a human resources executive and chief administrator and compelled her to chronicle her life's journey toward transformation in her book, *I Am Not Garbage*. From there, God has opened numerous doors for her and established several partnerships that allow her to minister the gospel of transformation and the word in general to multiple youth and women's organizations, social clubs, schools, and churches.

Today, Rein spends her time in servitude to Christ through

full-time ministry, and after joining in holy matrimony she has become prophetess and co-pastor alongside her husband, Apostle Derrick Wallace, for Greater Deliverance Global Ministries based in Atlanta, GA with churches also planted in California, Africa, Asia, and the Middle East. Prophetess Rein is a dynamic praise and worship leader, an author, a youth, family, and parent coach, a life coach, a spiritual coach, a mentor, and a highly sought-after motivational speaker, revivalist, prophetess, and preacher who is committed to leading others in the direction of wholeness, transformation, and freedom through the work of her organization Transformation University, her "Say Something Campaign," a campaign that encourages others to put a voice to their pain with the end goal of healing and transformation and through her Virtual Transformation Training Center, an online mentoring and membership program. Rein reaches many through transparent testimony, speaking engagements, classes, webinars, music, devotionals, books, and social and other media as a means of drawing others into their complete wholeness and transformation—teaching principles of living healthy and wholesome lives free from the pain of the past. She is also the proud mother of three beautiful boys, Paris, Pierre, and Caleb-Lyric.

Contact Prophetess Rein via email:
Bookprophetessrein@gmail.com

and visit her website:
www.reinwallaceministriesinternational.com

REIN'S ACKNOWLEDGEMENTS:

I bless God for being my Sovereign and my Soldier. You are my constant in a world of uncertainty.

To my family, my husband and children, thank you for being my rock and my reasons. Your endless support and push means the world to me.